A WEEKEND WITH REMBRANDT

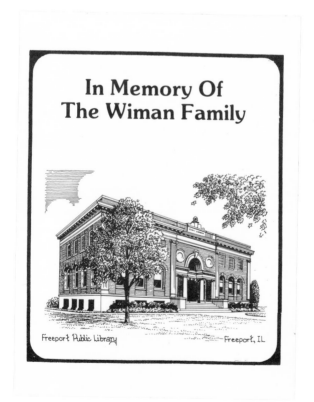

A WEEKEND WITH
REMBRANDT

by Pascal Bonafoux

SKIRA
RIZZOLI
NEW YORK

935195

It's the weekend. And on weekends, when I have finished praying at my church, the Westerkerk, people greet me as I walk down the the Rozengracht, the street along the canal where I have lived since 1660. They respect me. But it's not respect that makes them keep their distance from me—it's fear. They think I'm embittered, sad, and grouchy. But since nobody dares to disturb me, I can spend all my time painting. For painting, you see, is my whole life. *Who* am I, you ask? I am

Rembrandt

7

I've painted all my life, and I've never wanted to do anything else but paint. Let me tell you a story. A long time ago—a very long time ago—there was a painter in Greece by the name of Zeuxis. The paintings that he made were so wonderful that he was very famous. They say that he painted grapes so perfectly that birds would think they were real and try to peck at them! One day, an old woman came to see him to ask him to paint a portrait of Venus, the goddess of love and beauty. Zeuxis—he was as old as I am, sixty-one—agreed. Then the old woman demanded that she should be the model for the young goddess. And Zeuxis agreed to this, too. But then, when he was working on the painting, the situation seemed so ridiculous that he burst into laughter. And he laughed so hard that he died! Now there is not a single painting left by Zeuxis, not even a drawing, and yet people remember him as a great painter. And one day perhaps it will be the same for me: no one will know anymore what I painted. But they will know one thing, and that is that Rembrandt was a very great painter.

These faces, one titled Rembrandt Laughing, *and another which is called* Rembrandt Surprised, *are etchings, or prints, made when he was twenty-four years old. But these two self-portraits are certainly not the last. Rembrandt never stopped looking at himself in the mirror. Drawing himself, painting himself, engraving himself. . . .*

The city of Leiden, where I was born

Here is Leiden, where Rembrandt van Rijn was born on July 15, 1606. One of these windmills may well be the very one his father owned. Windmills were used to grind grain into flour, although sometimes, if there was a fire, they were used to pump water to put out the flames! Small boats navigated the canals that criss-crossed the countryside. Big ships sailed the oceans in all directions, to the East Indies (like Java and Sumatra) and to the West Indies (really the Americas).

Amsterdam, where I live now

Amsterdam, where Rembrandt spent his adult life, was at that time the biggest port in Europe. Along the docks you could find all sorts of things from the finest spices to the most exotic art objects. And because there was more tolerance here than anywhere else in Europe, and because one could have one's books printed here without having first to ask the king's permission, this city was the place where all the great philosophers, writers, and teachers of the time chose to live.

This canal is called the Singel; it is one of the main canals. Its name means "the belt," and it goes all the way around the city. Loaded cargo ships make their way around it ceaselessly. The seventeenth century is often called Amsterdam's Golden Age because several of the city's greatest painters lived during this period. It was also a time of enormous growth for the city. The population doubled in just a few years. New canals were dug. New bridges were built—more than six hundred of them.

There are more than six hundred bridges in my city

Now that I have introduced myself, I hope you can see that I may not be as grouchy as some people seem to think. I just have important things to consider. I'd like you to get to know my country. The land here is lower than the level of the sea, so dikes keep the water back. Sometimes people call it the "flat country" or the "low country." Here is a view of *The Curve of the Amstel, Near Kostverloren*. The Amstel is one of the most important canals in Amsterdam—in fact it is really a river that has been channeled into a canal running right through the city. When I follow it all the way, it takes me out to this broad countryside, which gives the impression of containing all the mysteries of the world within its vast expanse. Back in my studio, I take up my pad of drawing paper and quickly sketch the scene with my pen; then I add a few strokes with my paintbrush dipped in India ink—or I may choose "bistre," a gray-brown color, or some other color of ink—diluted with a little water.

The big river in my city

My wife Saskia and Me

Some people say that the young man raising his glass is the Biblical Prodigal Son who has just left his father's house with part of his inheritance. That is the religious interpretation, or meaning. But the face of the young man is Rembrandt's and the young woman's is that of Saskia, his wife. They had been married almost two years when it was painted. And it may well be that this painting is their response to those who criticized them for spending too much money and, among other extravagances, for living in a fine house that they had to borrow the money to buy.

Gold, tulips, and food

Gerrit Berckheyde and other Dutch painters who lived at the same time as Rembrandt loved to portray the prosperity of Amsterdam and the charm of the city's streets, canals, and gardens. This particular Flower Market *is one where the well-to-do people liked to go. There people bought, sold, and traded their foods, flowers, and other goods. All kinds of business deals and transactions could be overheard here...even concerning flowers. According to one writer of the period:*

> *Among the Dutch, during and following the year 1634, a singular trade in tulips developed. One could see wealthy business men deserting their offices and their shops just to cultivate tulips...and simple flowers sold like the most precious jewels and gemstones. One Dutchman gave for a single tulip, called the Viceroy, 36 setiers of wheat (a setier was an ancient measure for grain, amounting to over 100 bushels), 72 of rice, 12 sheep, and 8 pigs....*

This man who is making a list of his wealth and his treasures is considered one of the most important people in the city's administration. His name is Jan Uytenbogaert.

Fabrics, flowers, and feathers

I have rarely budged from my house. People have chided me about it because it is fashionable nowadays for artists in northern Europe to tour Italy—to journey through that country known for its great art treasures and study the work of the Italian masters. As for me, I've never had the time. First of all, I have to show people here that I am a great painter. And then they will understand that it's possible to be a great painter without having been to Italy. Anyway, with the engravings and reproductions I've bought, I'm familiar with all the Italian painters. I have all their works on my walls or in my notebooks and folders—all of them. If I am poor now, it's partly because of this. For the sake of painting, I have spent money without considering the price, buying books and paintings as well as weapons, precious fabrics, jewels. Now everything is gone—taken from me and sold at auction to pay my debts. . . .

This painting, Still Life with Two Dead Peacocks and a Girl, *reveals Rembrandt's technical mastery: the feathers have the color, light, and texture of silk. His taste for the most luxurious fabrics can be seen also in the* Portrait of Saskia Dressed as Flora, *the Roman goddess of flowers. Rembrandt loved his wife and liked to use her as his model. He draped her in shimmering silks and precious brocades, transforming her into countless roles and characters with these fabrics, with which his studio was filled. Here we see Saskia again, patient and attentive as always, seated next to her husband.*

For Rembrandt, everything he saw—objects, faces, costumes—inspired him to paint, engrave, and draw. He might make an etching of himself in a fur hat, or do a drawing of a Seashell; he might sketch the rags and tatters of a poor Blind Fiddler; or he might paint a portrait of the rich Amsterdam aristocrat Maerten Soolmans, elegantly dressed in velvet and lace. It made little difference to Rembrandt as long as he was working. Whatever subject he painted was metamorphosed, that is to say, was completely changed, or transformed by him. Rembrandt's ambition was not merely to have people recognize a face, a seashell, or an important personality, but to have them recognize that they were looking at "a Rembrandt"—a work of art by Rembrandt.

Rich man, poor man. . .

I know the anger and the shame felt by the very poor, whose desperate faces I have painted, just as I understand the vanity of some rich men whose portraits I have made. I also know what the children I draw are dreaming. And I'll tell you something more: paintings can not only show you who people are—men, women, and children and all their fears, their hopes, and dreams—but they can also help you understand practically everything. Here's the proof of it—look, really look, at this seashell, look at this beggar, look at this rich man. Now don't tell me you don't know who or what they are. If you look carefully at my paint-

ings, then, like me, you will see and understand the meaning of every glistening highlight, every muscle, every line and curve, and each reflection. I emphasize these things in my art to tell you how I see them and how you can see them, too. Does what I say seem to you a bit crazy? Or certainly ambitious? Well, you are not mistaken. I have always been ambitious. But my ambition keeps changing. First, I was ambitious *to* paint. But later, I was ambitious *for* the art of painting. You don't understand the difference? I'll explain it to you. . . .

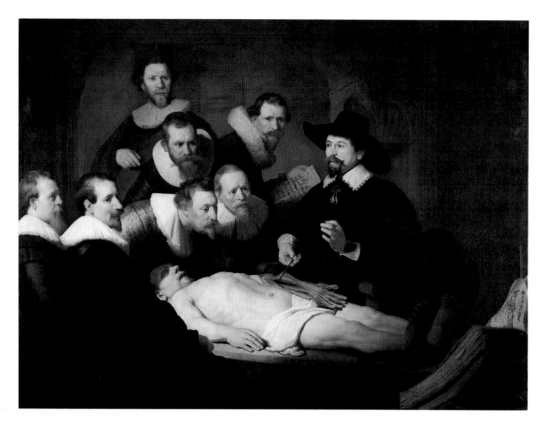

The Anatomy Lesson of Dr. Tulp

The Syndics of the Clothmakers' Guild

Rembrandt, the noted painter

Here, take a look at these two canvases I've painted, two group portraits. The first is called *The Anatomy Lesson of Dr. Tulp*. I painted this one in 1632. The second one is *The Syndics of the Clothmakers' Guild*. I painted this one in 1662. Look. In 1632, just one year after my arrival in Amsterdam, I received a commission, or order, from Dr. Tulp for a painting that I hoped would establish my reputation as an artist. I painted this first subject in such a way that you can look directly at it. I wanted people to see that no one could fulfill this kind of an order as well as I could, and I hoped to receive many more orders. Whereas, to look at the later painting, you have to raise your eyes—do you see how I have placed the table in front?—to pay homage, or respect, to the art of painting itself. In the first, you know the name of each person and just what he is doing. I painted it for them and for people like themselves. In the second painting, it is not so clear just who these people are—these board members—or why they are there together. It is for the sake of painting—for art's sake—that I have painted them. The first picture is about people—the second is about painting. People usually don't pay much attention to this difference. Perhaps they don't really know what painting is. But if you find it interesting to look for a long time at a painting—even though you don't know the people in the picture or what they are doing—well, there you have it! You are looking at painting!

The Nightwatch

Here is another story: I painted this picture in 1642. It is called *The Militia Company of Captain Frans Banning Cocq,* but it is more often referred to as *The Nightwatch*. These men with their drums, their swords, their guns, and their halberds are just going off to a battle exercise. When I painted this, our country was at peace. But before this we had been at war for a long time against Spain because Spain's people are Catholics and we Hollanders are Protestants. For many centuries religious differences caused strife among a number of countries. Is it like that in your country or elsewhere in your world?

For a long time now, men have liked to be painted in their military uniforms. It's become a tradition. So, of course, I was asked to do what everyone had always done. And for this, each member of the militia company of Captain Cocq (a very important citizen of Amsterdam) had paid me. But, look, there is a little rascal, with his head almost buried in a helmet, running away at the left; a little girl with a chicken hanging from her sash; and a dog barking at the drummer—you can guess that I didn't make *them* pay! When those who had posed for me saw

these scamps and also saw that I had dared to hide half of the face of one of the officers, they were astonished. But this was not what upset them the most; it was the movement and the lighting. They had assumed that I would paint them all lined up stiffly like a row of onions, one beside the other, each one posed in the most flattering way. What I delivered was not at all what they had expect-

ed! What's more, they couldn't see why, for example, the little girl is well-lighted but the gloved hand of Cocq, just in front of her, is in shadow. They didn't understand how the light could be so strong in some places and yet leave so many things in the shade. I'll tell you something that they didn't know: this kind of lighting exists only in my painting. This lighting is pure invention—I created it. For painting can show you what no one could ever see if the painting didn't exist.

The Militia Company of Captain Frans Banning Cocq, *also called* The Nightwatch, *only received the latter name during the nineteenth century. But that didn't keep it from being, along with Leonardo da Vinci's* La Gioconda *(better known as* Mona Lisa*), one of the most famous paintings in the world. Oddly enough, neither of these paintings now bears its original name. The Kloveniersdoelen, shown in the print below, was the general headquarters of Amsterdam's municipal guards. This was where Rembrandt's painting was hung. In 1715, the picture was moved to the City Hall; in order to get it through the two doors, the movers didn't hesitate to cut off an inch or so at left and right, and top and bottom! Since the end of the last century, it has hung in the Rijksmuseum in Amsterdam—where it still can be seen today.*

Remarkable scenes and stories from the Bible

Rembrandt often drew, painted, or engraved subjects taken from episodes in the Bible, but he always marked them with his own experience and personality. Here, he shows Abraham and Isaac, *like any father talking to his son—calmly, seriously. Below, in* Samson Threatening His Father-in-Law, *Rembrandt seems to have been mainly concerned with the extraordinary lighting. Probably he himself was the model for the angry man in this picture. As for the man in oriental costume (opposite) who seems curious about something just outside of the page, he is from the etching* The Descent from the Cross. *And again, Rembrandt probably based this on his own figure.*

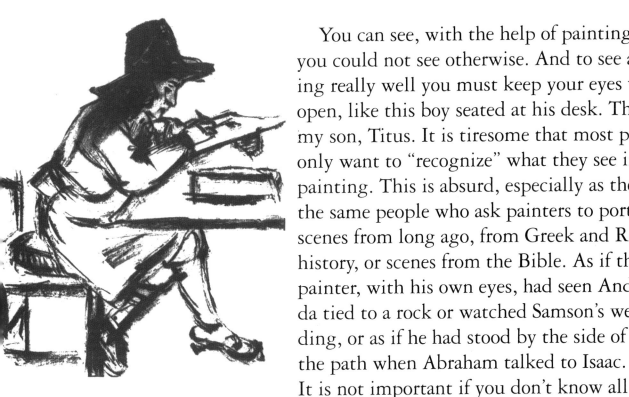

You can see, with the help of painting, what you could not see otherwise. And to see a painting really well you must keep your eyes wide open, like this boy seated at his desk. This is my son, Titus. It is tiresome that most people only want to "recognize" what they see in a painting. This is absurd, especially as these are the same people who ask painters to portray scenes from long ago, from Greek and Roman history, or scenes from the Bible. As if the painter, with his own eyes, had seen Andromeda tied to a rock or watched Samson's wedding, or as if he had stood by the side of the path when Abraham talked to Isaac. It is not important if you don't know all these people I am talking about; it's enough to know that they are heroes of legends, or people who really lived, but long ago, perhaps thousands of years ago. So neither you nor I could possibly know what they were truly like. But the funny thing is that, after I had painted Andromeda, Samson, Abraham and scores of other people whom I had never seen, the people who bought the canvases recognized them! Or, in fact, recognized the stories they had heard or read about.

Dreams of voyages to the East Indies

But I wanted them to accept a painting of something they had never seen before or of a story they did not know. That is why I painted many people the way I painted this man. He is wearing an oriental costume, but one can't tell what period he lived in, or what he is doing. When you know nothing about a person whose portrait you are looking at, then you can see it better as a painting. When people stop and look at a painting, they can imagine their own story. If they can't, well, then I insist that the painting doesn't exist—that it isn't a real painting.

The sailing ships that returned to Amsterdam from the ends of the world brought back rare spices—and also wild animals. See the Lion Devouring A Bird *or the* Elephant. *Of course, Rembrandt would delight in this chance to draw them from real life. To do this, he used a special kind of a black crayon: a stick of very dense black clay with which he could produce a wide range of tones from the deepest darks to the most subtle grays. This material, which has been used for many years in Italy, enables an artist to capture various effects of light and shadow, especially if it is heightened with the use of wash, as it is here. ("Wash" is the term for the use of water mixed with ink or pigment to produce a transparent effect.)*

My lively studio

The painter's studio is a magical place, and a subject which artists over the centuries have enjoyed portraying. And so did Rembrandt. This large drawing in bistre (gray-brown) ink is simply called The Artist in His Studio. The engraving opposite is said to be the studio of the great painter Jan van Eyck. He was a fifteenth-century Flemish master who invented the technique of painting in oils. We can see an apprentice grinding pigments (colors) in a mortar and another cleaning a palette (a board on which colors are mixed). There is a student copying a bust, another one working on a large canvas, and another sketching the outlines for a portrait of a woman. Rembrandt's studio would not have been very different from this one. The sketch shown on the preceding two pages gives you a good idea of how it looked. This was probably drawn by one of Rembrandt's pupils, of whom he had many. Probably his studio was messier than this—one observer wrote that Rembrandt "had a careless and dirty appearance" which was "the result of a habit he had, when painting, of wiping his brushes on his clothes."

The work of a painter

The work of a printmaker

Not content with painting for the great glory of painting, I have also done many prints. Prints are the best means of making yourself known, as you can make many impressions, or copies, of a single print. For, instead of drawing a picture on paper, you draw it on a flat sheet of copper (1). Your picture may be drawn by scratching it into the copper plate with a very sharp tool called a "burin" or you can coat the surface of the plate with a waxlike substance and draw on that. In the latter case, the plate will then be placed completely in acid, which will eat away the metal where you have marked it (2). Now you cover it with ink (3), and then carefully clean the surface, leaving the ink only in the crevices made by the drawing. Next, put a piece of paper on it and press it carefully down on the plate. The ink will stick to the paper, which you then remove carefully (4). Your drawing will be reproduced on the paper. This is called "pulling a proof" or a print. You can make as many as you want, until the plate is worn out. Very few people are able to come to see my paintings. But prints of my engravings or etchings (a special kind of engraving) can be bought by everyone in the world.

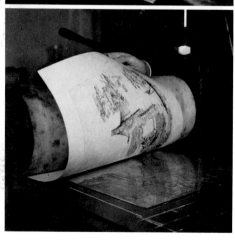

Caspar Luyken, a Dutch engraver from the end of the seventeenth century, shows (opposite) how to pull a proof with an Arm Press. *The heavy roller presses the paper smoothly against the plate. Then the prints were hung up like laundry while the ink dried.*

A windmill, an etching, a frame

Let us imagine that you could frame this etching and hang it on your wall, so you could look at it for a long time. Each day you would discover a new detail, some feature you had overlooked before. It would not be surprising if, after a while, you thought this might be a picture of the house that belonged to Rembrandt's grandfather, who also owned a Windmill. But even if that turned out not to be the case, what difference would it make? Rembrandt loved this kind of scene, so typical of the countryside just outside of Amsterdam: immense landscapes open to the horizon, flat fields punctuated by windmills with their big blades, which could be seen from afar, signaling the presence of stocky, thatch-roofed farmhouses. Especially in the last fifteen years of his life, Rembrandt returned again and again to this area, where he made many drawings and etchings and also some paintings.

...wide lace collars

You must have admired, on the two preceding pages, the two splendid portraits. On the left is that of Agatha Bas, *a rich merchant's daughter, painted in 1641. At right, dated 1639, is the portrait of* Maria Trip, *daughter of the burgomaster of Amsterdam. The burgomaster was the master of the burg, or city— the mayor. Rembrandt's taste for golden ornaments and luxurious clothing was undeniable. Look carefully at this picture of King Ozias, stricken with leprosy. Ozias, or Azarius, tenth king of Judea, lived, according to the Bible, in the eighth century* B.C. *His reign marked the end of an era of prosperity for the Jews. Look at the detail of the beautiful fasteners on his cloak. Then turn the page and look at the extraordinary harmony of the hands and the brilliance of the fabrics which make a sort of musical accompaniment to this moving painting,* The Jewish Bride, *(as it has long been called, although no one really knows precisely why).*

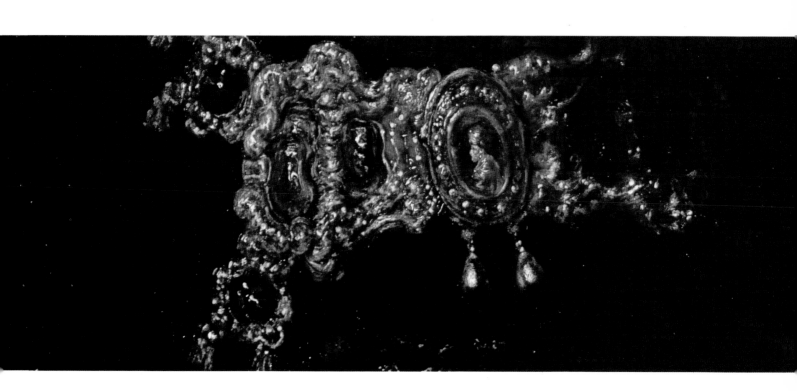

I've been painting for more than forty years. In those years I have painted or drawn or engraved just about everything. I had all the work I wanted. But now my luck has changed. The rich people of Amsterdam, who gave me the portrait commissions from which I made my living, have cooled toward me. However, I'm not sad about that—nor grouchy, either! Not at all! For, would you believe just a few days ago, I heard from the Grand Duke of Tuscany— that he is coming to see me next Thursday? To see *me,* considered a nobody by the wealthy men of Amsterdam. The Grand Duke of Tuscany is coming to see *me,* Rembrandt! And he is coming all the way from Italy, from the land of the great master artists, where I have never been! And who knows? Maybe he'll buy a painting. Or perhaps commission a new one!

No doubt you have noticed that I have often used myself as a model. That is because, if I paint myself, I don't have to account to anyone for what I paint. My self-portraits don't reveal anything except that I am a painter, nothing else but a painter. It is through painting alone that I show my spirit. How does painting portray my spirit? I'll show you. Look. Look at the tenderness of this man's gesture towards the young woman at his side. See how exquisitely their clothes are painted, and their faces. Look carefully at his sleeve, so delicate it might be made of light. It is with things like this—incomparable, indescribable things— that painting reveals my spirit. If you go to see all my paintings, the ones that I have sold, the ones that are no longer here in my studio, then you will understand what I mean. It is with my paint- brushes, my pencils, and my burins that I have prayed, that I have spoken, that I have loved.

Now, I must prepare for the Grand Duke. But, on second thought, he can wait. What else would you like to know?

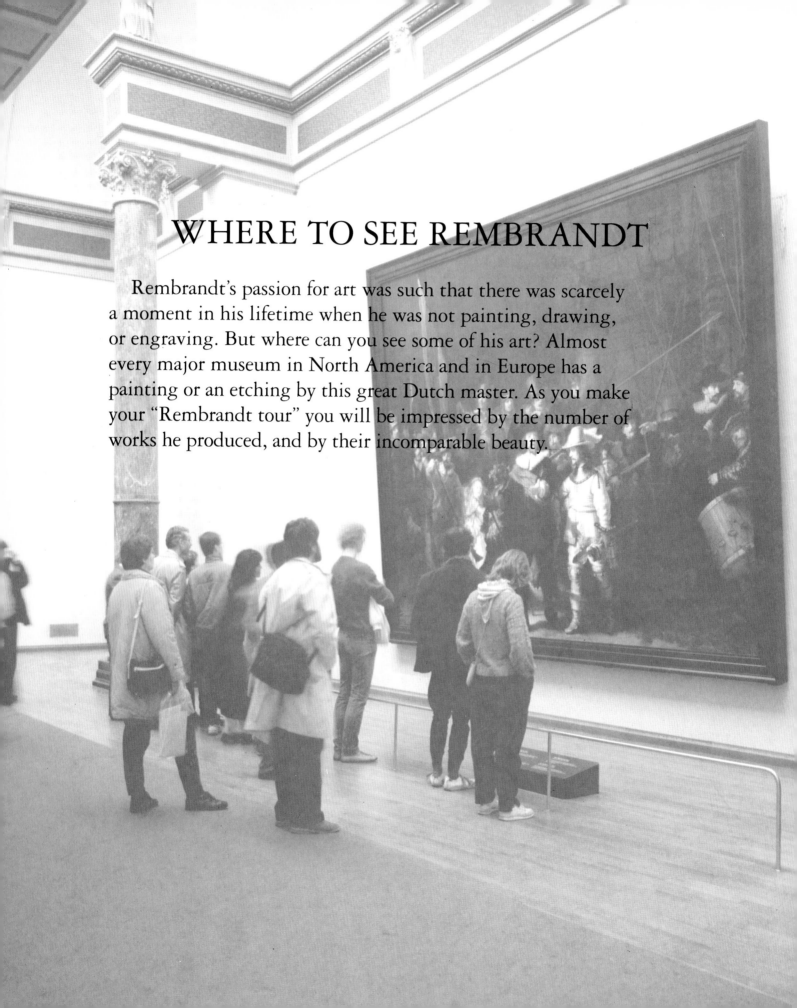

WHERE TO SEE REMBRANDT

Rembrandt's passion for art was such that there was scarcely a moment in his lifetime when he was not painting, drawing, or engraving. But where can you see some of his art? Almost every major museum in North America and in Europe has a painting or an etching by this great Dutch master. As you make your "Rembrandt tour" you will be impressed by the number of works he produced, and by their incomparable beauty.

New York
The Metropolitan Museum of Art

This wonderful museum has one of the biggest collections of art treasures in the world. To see everything on display would take you many weeks or months of study. But if you go straight up the great outdoor staircase, walk though the front door and across the marbled hallway and then climb up another large staircase, you will come right to the rooms where Rembrandt's paintings are. And what paintings they are! One of the most famous is the one showing *Aristotle with a Bust of Homer*. There is a fine *Self-Portrait*, and many other portraits, including the dramatic *Noble Slav*. There are also many fine drawings and etchings.

The Frick Collection

One of Rembrandt's most appealing paintings, *The Polish Rider*, can be seen in this museum, which was once the home of steel baron Henry Clay Frick. The sensitive face of the horseman, and his aristocratic bearing seem to indicate that he is a nobleman—but no one has discovered who he is or where he is going—it is still an intriguing mystery. Here, too, you can see another *Self-Portrait*.

The Pierpont Morgan Library

Among the many art treasures collected by financier Pierpont Morgan are some of Rembrandt's finest etchings of various subjects, including *Christ Preaching*, *Christ Healing the Sick*, several *Self-Portraits* (including those on page 3 of this book), and portraits of *Rembrandt's Mother* and *Rembrandt's Father*.

Washington, D.C.
The National Gallery of Art

A visit to this great museum is bound to be a highlight of any trip to the nation's capital. And, as you might expect, you will find here a number of Rembrandt's finest paintings. There are three fine *Self-Portraits* from different periods; a lovely landscape painting, *The Mill*; and several portraits, including what many people consider to be his best, the beautiful *Lady with an Ostrich Feather Fan.*

Boston, Massachusetts

In this city you can see the striking portrait of Pastor Johannes Elison as well as the early *Artist in His Studio* at the Museum of Fine Arts. And at the Isabella Stewart Gardner Museum is another very fine *Self-Portrait,* as well as other portraits by Rembrandt.

Chicago, Illinois
The Art Institute of Chicago

Here you can see *Old Man with Gorget and Cap* and a very good *Portrait of the Artist's Mother.* There is also the appealing painting of a *Young Girl at an Open Half-Door.* The balance of the curves of the girl's figure with the rectangles of the doorway are unusual for Rembrandt; perhaps he had been studying the compositions of some of the Italian painters of the period when he did this painting. Here you can also see some of his etchings and engravings.

Other Parts of the United States and Canada

There are excellent examples of Rembrandt's work in museums all over the country. In California, at the M.H. de Young Memorial Museum in San Francisco is the Portrait of Joris de Caullery; in Los Angeles at the J. Paul Getty Museum and the Los Angeles County Museum of Art there are also works by Rembrandt.

You can see others at The Detroit Institute of Arts, as well as at The Houston Museum of Fine Arts, The Cleveland Museum of Art, the Philadelphia Museum of Art, The Fine Arts Museum of San Francisco, The Indianapolis Museum of Art and the National Gallery of Canada.

In Other Parts of the World

Amsterdam, The Netherlands (Holland)

In Europe, one thinks first of Amsterdam as the place in which to see Rembrandt's art. And rightly so. In the distinctive shapes of its houses, in the reflections in its canals, this city has retained a special atmosphere that evokes echoes of the footsteps of this famous artist. A visit to the Rijksmuseum (National Museum) is an ideal way to begin the European part of your Rembrandt tour. Here, displayed as the jewel of the museum's collection, you may see Rembrandt's best-known painting, *The Nightwatch* (pages 26 and 27 of this book). And among other masterpieces, you must not miss *The Syndics of the Clothmakers' Guild* (page 24) and *The Jewish Bride* (page 47). You'll also want to visit Rembrandthuis—the house where Rembrandt and Saskia lived. His studio is still there, with furniture of the period, as well as his old press for pulling proofs, and his engraver's tools.

The Hague, The Netherlands (Holland)
Mauritshuis Museum

The Hague is another historic Dutch city, now well known all over the world as the seat of the International Court of Justice. In the two "Rembrandt Rooms" of the former palace that is now the Mauritshuis Museum are some of the master's most famous works. There is *The Anatomy Lesson of Dr. Tulp* (page 24) which was the first commission the painter received for a group portrait. There are also several fine *Self-Portraits:* in one he is still young; in another, he is more mature, with a proud expression, wearing a large, feather-trimmed velvet beret; and in still another, he looks out at us with a somber, weary gaze. And there are also some of his extraordinary paintings of scenes from the Bible, including the stunning *David Playing the Harp for Saul* and *Susanna and the Elders*.

Paris
The Louvre Museum

The Louvre is the biggest museum in France. Of course you will not find here, as you can find in Holland, the atmosphere of the period when Rembrandt lived and worked. But you can see many of his important works: several *Self-Portraits*, a *Portrait of Titus*, and a *Portrait of Hendrickje*, several biblical scenes and also *The Skinned Ox*.

London
The National Gallery

The museums of England are rich with artistic treasures. Naturally, Rembrandt is well-represented here—there are twenty works in this collection alone. The serene half-smile of *Hendrickje Bathing in a River*; the altar gleaming in a shaft of golden light in *Christ with the Adulteress*; the brilliance of the proud, deeply lined face, rising above a broad, embroidered collar, of the old woman Marguerite Trip—these are some of the marvelous visions that will linger in your memory after a visit to this fabulous museum.

Berlin
Gemäldegalerie Staatliche Museun

Germany also possesses some of Rembrandt's masterpieces. In the eighteenth century, Frederick the Great, King of Prussia (1712–1786), a lover of all the arts, set up the first German collection of paintings in this gallery. Here you may see one of the paintings that some experts claim may not have been painted entirely by Rembrandt—*The Golden*

Helmet. You can also see some of the wonderful examples of Rembrandt's use of chiaroscuro, the dramatic use of light and shadow so typical of this artist, as in the *Portrait of Cornelis Anslo,* or in the angry expression of *Samson Threatening His Father-in-Law* (seen on page 30).

Kassel
Gemäldegalerie Staatliche Kunstsammlungen

Kassel is a large German city. Its museum contains, among other Rembrandts, a *Portrait of Saskia,* sumptuously dressed and wearing a lot of gold jewelry. Shown in profile, she wears the feather-trimmed velvet beret which the painter liked so much.

Russia

If your Rembrandt tour can extend to this country, you must not overlook the Pushkin Museum in Moscow and, above all, the Hermitage Museum in St. Petersburg. Both have a considerable number of very beautiful paintings by Rembrandt, including *David and Uriah, Portrait of Saskia Dressed as Flora,* and *Abraham's Sacrifice.*

IMPORTANT DATES IN THE LIFE OF
REMBRANDT

1606– 1669	*Rembrandt lived in the seventeenth century, during a period that is considered the Golden Age of Holland. This era saw the rise of a class of merchants and businessmen whose commerce carried them to all parts of the world. Rich and open to new ideas—for instance, they welcomed the great philosopher Descartes who was tired of the criticism he received in his own country of France—these wealthy men were also lovers of art, and thus commissioned a remarkable number of individual and group portraits, thus enabling the painters of this period and place to live very well.*
1606	Rembrandt Harmenzoon (son of Harmen) van Rijn is born in the university city of Leiden in Holland (The Netherlands). His father is a miller, owner of a large and busy windmill.
1620– 1623	After attending the university for a few months, he leaves to be an apprentice and to study art. The two studios in which he works are both run by artists who had studied for long periods in Italy, but Rembrandt himself never goes there. This is unusual because a tour of Italy was at that time considered an essential part of an artist's training.
1624	Rembrandt works for six months in Amsterdam with Lastman, who is well known as a painter of historical scenes and who probably met or studied with Caravaggio in Italy. On his return to Leiden, Rembrandt opens his own studio which he shares with the painter Lievens, the son of an embroiderer. He begins work as an engraver; Lievens and he soon become part of a circle of intellectuals and art lovers. Through the recommendations of jurist and poet Constantin Huygens, Rembrandt receives orders for several paintings.
1631	He goes to live in Amsterdam, where he becomes associated with the art dealer Hendrick van Uylenburch, in whose house he opens a studio and meets Saskia, his future wife.

1634   In July he marries. His beautiful bride, Saskia, is the niece of his art dealer and landlord, and the daughter of a man who has held several high government posts. She brings a substantial dowry to the marriage.

1639–
1641   He buys a very large and expensive house in which he accumulates a collection of rich fabrics, jewels, weapons, sculpture, and paintings. Among these, for example, is one of Raphael's most famous portraits, which is now in the Louvre; he also has an equally celebrated painting by Titian, which now hangs in the National Gallery in London. He works very hard; this is the happiest period of his life, crowned, in 1641, by the birth of his son Titus, whom he dearly loves and often paints.

1642   Saskia dies in June. In this same year he finishes The Nightwatch, commissioned for the headquarters of the municipal guard, which will become one of the most famous paintings in the world.

1649–
1653   The young peasant girl Hendrickje Stoffels joins the household; hired to take care of Titus. Hendrickje is a faithful companion to both father and son, seeing them through many difficult times. Rembrandt often paints her pleasant features, with her simple, tranquil expression. But in spite of the many commissions he still receives, and his great ability and fame, he seems distraught. Once wealthy, his uncontrolled extravagances finally swallow up all of his money.

1654–
1656   Rembrandt and Hendrickje have a daughter, whom he names Cornelia. Little by little, his finances deteriorate until finally he is near bankruptcy. All of his possessions have to be sold to pay his creditors, including seventy of his paintings, his house, and his furniture.

1660–
1669   With Hendrickje, little Cornelia and Titus, he goes to live in a modest house in a less elegant part of the city. But in spite of everything, he continues to work very hard and to enjoy considerable prestige. The Grand Duke Cosimo de Medici III comes to visit him. After the deaths of Hendrickje and Titus, Rembrandt becomes more solitary and lonely despite the presence of little Cornelia.

1669   Rembrandt dies.

TABLE OF ILLUSTRATIONS

The list that follows tells the title, medium and date of works reproduced in this book as well as where they can be found. Dimensions are given, height by width, in inches and centimeters. Unless otherwise specified, photographs are archival documents.

Cover

Self-Portrait as Apostle Paul. 1661. Oil on canvas, 36⅛ x 30⅜" (79.4 x 77 cm.). Amsterdam, Rijksmuseum.

Pages 4–5

Meadow with a Windmill, at the Edge of Town. About 1641. Pen and ink with bistre wash, 5½ x 11⅜" (14.2 x 28.8 cm.). Chantilly, Musée Condé (Photograph by Giraudon).

Page 6

Self-Portrait, detail. 1657. Oil on canvas, 19⅜ x 16¾" (50 x 42.5 cm.). Edinburgh, National Gallery of Scotland.

Page 6

Meadow with a Windmill, at the Edge of Town, details.

Page 7

Tower of the Westerkerk in Amsterdam, Seen from the Prinsengracht. About 1646. Pen and ink with bistre wash, 7½ x 5⅝" (19 x 14.8 cm.). Amsterdam, Stedelijk Museum.

Portrait of Saskia in a Straw Hat, detail. June 8, 1663. Silverpoint with inscription: "This is a drawing of my fiancée when she was twenty-one years old, three days after we announced our engagement." Berlin, Kupferstichkabinett.

Page 8

Rembrandt in a Cap, Laughing. 1630. Etching, 2⅛ x 2" (5.2 x 4.3 cm.). Amsterdam, Rijksmuseum.

Pages 8–9

Rembrandt in a Cap, Surprised, enlarged. 1630. Etching, 2⅛ x 2" (5.1 x 4.6 cm.). Amsterdam, Rijksmuseum.

Page 10

View of Leyden, by Peter Bast, detail. 1601. Engraving, 3 x 8" (7 x 18 cm.). London, British Museum. (Museum photograph).

Page 11

Panoramic View of Amsterdam. Engraving from *Wegwyzer door Amsterdam,* published in Amsterdam in 1713. Private collection.

Pages 10–11

Study of a Young Man Pulling a Rope. About 1636. Pen, brush, and wash, 13 x 8" (29 x 17.8 cm.). Amsterdam, Rijksmuseum, Rijksprentenkabinet.

Pages 12–13

The Singel, Amsterdam, by Reiner Nooms Zeeman, enlarged. Engraving, 6 x 11" (13.5 x 24.7 cm.). London, British Museum. (Museum photograph).

Pages 14–15

The Curve of the Amstel, Near Kostverloren. About 1648–50. Pen and wash, 6½ x 12" (14.5 x 26.9 cm.). Paris, Musée du Louvre. Rothschild donation. (Photograph by Giradon).

Page 16

A Section of Amsterdam. Engraving taken from *Wegwyzer door Amsterdam,* published in Amsterdam in 1713. Private collection.

Page 17

Portrait of the Artist with Saskia or *The Prodigal Son.* 1634/35 or 36. Oil on canvas, 63⅜ x 51½" (161 x 131 cm.). Dresden, Staatliche Kunstsammlungen.

Page 18

Tulips: Genevieve, Queen Nina. Colored engraving from Charles Malo, *The History of Tulips* (1830). Private collection.

The Flower Market in Amsterdam, by Gerrit Adriaensz Berckheyde 1673. Oil on canvas, 17¾ x 24" (45 x 61 cm.). Amsterdam, Rijksmuseum. (Museum photograph).

Page 19

Jan Uytenbogaert, Tax Collector. 1639. Etching. (25 x 20.4 cm.). Amsterdam, Rijksmuseum. (Musuem photograph).

Page 20

Still Life with Two Dead Peacocks and a Girl. 1637. Oil on canvas, 57 x 53⅜" (145 x 135.5 cm.). Amsterdam, Rijksmuseum. (Museum photograph).

Page 21

Portrait of Saskia Dressed as Flora, detail. 1634. Oil on canvas, 49 x 40" (125 x 101 cm.).
St. Petersburg, Hermitage Museum. Photograph André Held, Ecublens).

Self-Portrait with Saskia. 1636. Etching, 4 x 3¾" (10.4 x 9.5 cm.). Amsterdam, Rijksmuseum.
(Museum photograph).

Pages 22–23

The Blind Fiddler, detail, enlarged. 1631. Etching, 3 x 2" (7.9 x 5.4 cm.) Paris, Bibliothèque
Nationale, Print Collection. (Museum photograph).

The Seashell, detail. 1650. Drypoint and burin, 3¾ x 5⅛" (9.7 x 13.2 cm.). Amsterdam,
Rijksmuseum. (Museum photograph).

Rembrandt in Fur Hat and Light Dress. 1630. Etching, 3⅝ x 2¾" (9.2 x 7 cm.). Amsterdam,
Rijksmuseum. (Museum photograph).

Portrait of Maerten Soolmans. 1634. Oil on canvas, 82¾ x 53⅛" (210 x 135 cm.). Private collection.

Page 24

The Anatomy Lesson of Dr. Tulp. 1632. Oil on canvas, 66½ x 85¼" (169 x 216.6 cm.). The Hague,
Mauritshuis. (Photograph André Held, Ecublens).

The Syndics of the Clothmakers' Guild. 1662. Oil on canvas, 75⅜ x 110¼" (191 x 279 cm.).
Amsterdam, Rijksmuseum. (Photograph André Held, Ecublens).

Page 25

Rembrandt Standing, in His Painter's Smock. 1655. Ink, 8 x 5¼" (20.3 x 13.4 cm.) Amsterdam,
Rembrandt House. (Museum photograph).

Pages 26–27

The Nightwatch or *The Militia Company of Captain Frans Banning Cocq.* 1642. Oil on canvas, 141⅜ x
172⅜" (359 x 438 cm.). Amsterdam, Rijksmuseum. (Museum photograph).

Page 28

The Nightwatch, details.

Page 29

The Kloveniersdoelen in Amsterdam by Jacob van Meurs. Engraving, 10 x 8" (25.3 x 20.3 cm.). London,
British Library. (Photograph British Library).

Page 30

Abraham and Isaac. 1645. Etching. Geneva, Print Collection. (Photograph Fred Pillonel).

Samson Threatening His Father-in-Law. 1635. Oil on canvas, 60¾ x 50⅞" (156 x 129 cm.). Berlin,
Gemäldegalerie, Staatliche Museen Preussicher Kulturbesitz. (Museum photograph).

Page 31

Young Boy Drawing at a Desk (probably Titus). About 1655/56. Pen and brush. Dresden, Kupferstichkabinett.

The Descent from the Cross, detail. 1633. Etching. Amsterdam, Rijksmuseum.

Page 32

Lion Devouring a Bird. 1637. Crayon and wash, 4¾ x 5½" (12 x 14 cm.). London, British Museum.

Elephant. 1637. Crayon, 9 x 13⅜" (23 x 34 cm.). Vienna, Albertina Museum.

Page 33

Standing Man in Oriental Costume. About 1633. Pen and ink and wash, 8¾ x 6¾" (22 x 16.9 cm.). London, British Museum.

Pages 34–35

Rembrandt Seated Among His Students Drawing a Nude by an anonymous student of Rembrandt. Pen and sepia ink, 7 x 12½" (18.0 x 31.7 cm.). Weimar, Kunstsammlungen zu Weimar. (Museum photograph).

Page 36

Mortars and Palette. Illustrations from *Petit Larousse Illustré.*

Artist in His Studio. 1632/33. Ink and bistre, 8 x 6¾" (20.5 x 17 cm.). Malibu, J. Paul Getty Museum.

Page 37

The Artist in His Studio, said to be the studio of Jan van Eyck, by Jay van Straet (Stradanus). Engraved by Theodor Galle. 17th century. Paris, Reunion des Musées Nationaux. (Photograph RMN).

Page 38

Different Steps in Engraving. Photographs taken from *Rembrandt Etchings and Drawings in Rembrandt House.*

Page 39

Workshop and Arm-Press by Caspar Luyken, enlarged. 1698. Etching, 3⅜ x 3" (8.6 x 7.8 cm.). Fribourg, Musée d'Art et d'Histoire. (Museum photograph).

Pages 40–41

The Windmill. 1641. Etching. Amsterdam, Rembrandt House (Museum photograph).

Page 42

Portrait of Agatha Bas, Wife of Nicolas van Bambeeck. 1641. Oil on canvas, 41½ x 33" (105.5 x 84 cm.). Copyright © by Her Majesty Queen Elizabeth II. London, Buckingham Palace, The Royal Collection (Photograph Royal Collection).

Page 43

Portrait of Maria Trip. 1639. Oil on canvas, 42⅛ x 32¼" (107 x 82 cm.). Amsterdam, Rijksmuseum. (Museum photograph).

Pages 44–45

King Ozias Stricken with Leprosy. 1635. Oil on canvas, 40 x 30⅜" (101.5 x 77 cm.). Chatsworth, Duke of Devonshire Collection.

Page 46

The Easel, detail. 1628. Oil on canvas, 9⅞ x 12½" (25.1 x 31.9 cm.). Boston, Museum of Fine Arts. (Museum photograph).

Page 47

The Jewish Bride, detail. 1665. Oil on canvas, 47¾ x 65⅝" (121 x 167 cm.). Amsterdam, Rijksmuseum. (Museum photograph).

Other books in the Weekend with Series

Picasso
Degas
Renoir

First published in the United States of America in 1992 by
Rizzoli International Publications, Inc.
300 Park Avenue South
New York, New York 10010

Library of Congress Cataloging-in-Publication Data

Bonafoux, Pascal.
    [Dimanche avec Rembrandt. English]
    A weekend with Rembrandt / by Pascal Bonafoux.
        p.   cm.
    Translation of: Un dimanche avec Rembrandt.
    Summary: The seventeenth-century Dutch painter talks about his
life and work as if entertaining the reader for the weekend.
Includes reproductions of the artist's works and a list of museums
where works are on display.
    ISBN 0-8478-1441-6
    1. Rembrandt Harmenszoon van Rijn, 1606–1669—Juvenile literature.
2. Artists—Netherlands—Biography—Juvenile literature.
[1. Rembrandt Harmenszoon van Rijn, 1606–1669. 2. Artists.]
    I. Title. II. Rembrandt
N6953.R4B6513.   1992
759.9492—dc20   91-40507
[B]   CIP
                                                     AC

Design by Mary McBride

Printed in Great Britain